A TREE IS A TIME MACHINE

ROB & TOM SEARS

LAURENCE KING

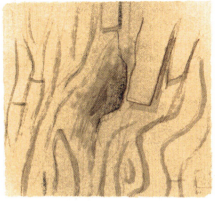

Do you ever think deep thoughts about time?

I do.

But then, I've had a lot of time to think them.

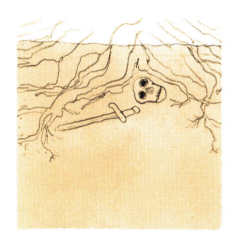

This is me.
I'm a yew tree.

You can call me Eunice.

A monk gave me that name
about 1,400 rings ago
(or 1,400 years, as
humans would say).

It really tickled his roots.

Sometimes people come and spend a few minutes with me.

I often try to share my ideas about my specialist subject, time.
But one thing I've discovered about humans . . .

is that you're always in a hurry.

So I promise not to ramble.
At least, not too much.

I'm around 4,000 years old.

I'm guessing you're younger. Your bark looks very smooth.

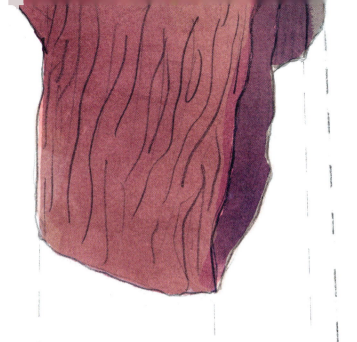

Actually, no one knows exactly
how old I am. My inner rings
have rotted away.

How I'd look if
someone sawed
through my trunk
(touch wood, this
will never happen)

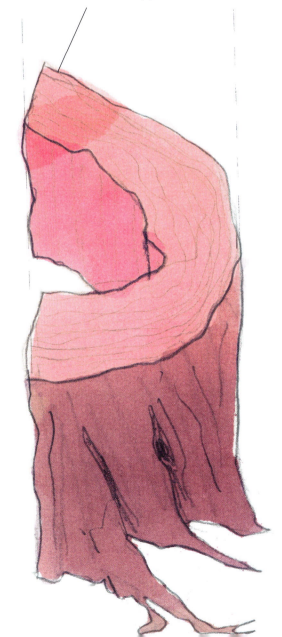

So let's just say I've been around for ages.

Bronze Age

Iron Age

Industrial Age　　　　　　　　Information Age

I'm so old, I've experienced all this:

1.5 million sunrises

20 lightning strikes

4 million dog pees

1,643 lost balls

72,103 bird's nests

1 epic battle between
a bear and an eagle

I'm so old, I'm older than all of these:

The English language

The Great Wall of China

The Inca Empire

The oldest known song

The domestic duck

Paper

I'm so old, I've known humans throughout history . . .

like the Druids who danced around me,

the Romans who marched past me,

the Vikings who camped under me,

the Normans who cut my wood to make longbows (not cool, Normans),

and the Victorians who strolled beneath my branches.

Then there was my best friend Joan.
We did everything together.

She's a bench now.

So I really am very, very, very old.

Or am I?

The hills over there are far more
ancient. So are the stones in the
soil around my roots.

An ordinary pebble—the kind you
step on every day without noticing—
could be 450 million years old.

In its long existence, it might
have been flung from a volcano,
washed across an ocean, frozen in
a glacier, and stepped on by herds
of dinosaurs.

And a pebble's long existence is short compared to the age of a much bigger rock—the planet itself.

Imagine that this branch of mine represents the entire history of Earth . . .

The planet formed out of swirling gas and dust here.

Early life appeared here.

5 billion years ago

4 billion years ago

3 billion years ago

At this point, Earth was almost totally frozen, but luckily it warmed up.

The first fungi grew here.

My great ancestor, the first tree, didn't appear until nine-tenths of the way through the planet's lifetime.

The first bird turned up here.

And humans didn't come on the scene until almost the tip of my farthest twig, 200,000 years ago.

2 billion years ago

1 billion years ago

Now

Woo-hoo!

Put another way: If Earth's history was a 24-hour party, people would only have dropped in at the very last second.

And even Earth is young compared
to some of the galaxies out in space.

Sometimes I let the starlight shower
down on me and think about all the
time that's gone by since the universe
began 14 billion years ago.

It's a funny feeling, gazing
into the deep past like this . . .
but I kind of like it.

Ever wanted to fly through time? Just look up. Many of the stars are so far away, it takes light thousands of years to get here, meaning that you're seeing them as they were long, long ago.
Wow!

In the distant past, there must have been centuries when it seemed as if nothing whatsoever was going on.

It wouldn't have seemed like much was happening in Earth's ancient rock pools, either.

But over millions and billions of years, new stars, planets, and galaxies were forming.

But over time, the first life forms were taking shape. And these tiny creatures slowly evolved into bigger ones.

What I'm saying is: Time is the secret of change. And that change has tended to be *reeeeaaally* slow. At least, until recently.

As far back as I can remember, humans have always been buzzy, fast-moving little creatures. They were always making changes to the place.

Like building burial mounds,

moving giant stones around,

turning meadows
into battlefields,

mowing grass with
their sheep,

or cutting down my fellow trees for firewood.

But like us plants, humans relied on the sun and seasons to set their schedules. And when the world slowed down in winter, so did they.

Until one day, something happened.

A clock appeared.

Now there were no excuses for a person to sleep in late or go to bed early.

In the age of clocks, people could organize to the minute when it was time to work, trade, pray, take part in a duel, or meet a friend under my branches.

Thou art three minutes late, Wilomena.

Three whats?

As the clocks ticked and tocked,
more changes came.

The piano,
1709

Gas lighting,
1807

The penny-farthing,
1871

The newspaper,
1605

Golf,
1744

Indoor plumbing,
1850s

The airship,
1900

The airplane,
1903

The quadcopter drone,
1991

The personal computer,
1981

PC

The automobile,
1886

The cell phone,
1983

The robot dog,
2005

It was as though a parade of new
inventions was marching beneath me.

And once the inventions spread, activities that used to take ages, like saying hi to your cousin living thousands of miles away . . .

could suddenly be done in no time at all.

For awhile, I figured that humans would use all the time they were saving to slow down and act more like trees.

Maybe they'd stand around, swaying in the breeze and relaxing, instead of zooming about the place.

I think I would have liked that.

But it didn't work out that way.

Today, humans can get around faster, communicate faster, make things faster, and throw them away faster, too.

So that's what most of them do.

Even if it doesn't always make them happy.

This is May, my mayfly pal.

Most of the time, she's just a blur, but if you can get her to slow down, she has some trunk-blowing stats to share . . .

May told me that every second, around the world, all this happens because of humans:

4 babies born

2 couples married

4 million emails sent

160 pizzas baked

3 bicycles manufactured

30 years of TV watched

3 vehicles built

28 tons of wheat grown

61,400 photos taken

6,000 rolls of toilet
tissue used

575 lb of chocolate made

1 plane takes off

100 people board roller coasters

But in the same second, all this happens because of humans, too:

44 tons of food wasted

74 tons of trash
thrown away

1,200 barrels of
oil burned

3 tons of clothes discarded

16,000 plastic
bags used

430 square feet of coral destroyed

40,000 square feet of land becomes desert

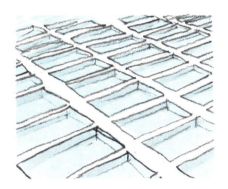

50 Olympic pools
of water used

7 tons of
fertilizer sprayed

26,460 tons of
ice melts

2 tons of electrical
goods thrown out

And it's happening . . . Every. Single. Second.

Worst of all, in about the time it takes for you
to read this sentence and turn the page . . .

. . . a whole football field
of forest gets cut
down.

When I start worrying about all this runaway change,
there's one thing that helps me.

I breathe slowly in and out of my needles.

 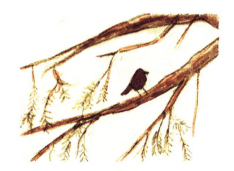 

I focus on what's happening in my branches
and roots in the present moment.

And I tune into tree time (the kind that's been
unfolding since long before clocks).

Until finally, I feel calm enough
to think about what comes next.

You're young.

You've only been on Earth for 200,000 years.

A typical species continues on for between
a million and ten million years—and
some last much longer.

T. REX (EXTINCT)
2.5 million years

BLUE WHALES
4.5 million years

WOOLLY MAMMOTH (EXTINCT)
5 million years

APPLE TREES
10 million years

GIRAFFE
1 million years

AUSTRALOPITHECUS
(EARLY HUMANS, EXTINCT)
900,000 years

HOMO SAPIENS (THAT'S YOU)
200,000 years and counting . . .

So, unless humans really mess things up,
you should have a long future to come.

With all this time ahead for the human race,
the other trees and I have a question for you . . .

WHAT'S

BIG

I know, it's easy for us to say. We're rooted to the spot.

Whereas, you have a million things you could be doing at any given moment.

And your lives aren't very long—at least by my standards.

The average person lives for only 4,000 weeks! That's as many needles as there are on this page.

No wonder you try to cram a lot in.

But 4,000 needles should still
be plenty of time to slow down
now and then.

Perhaps you could close your
eyes and daydream about the
kind of future you'd like to
build?

Here are some human seedlings—or babies, as you call them.

There are billions of these future people on the way.

And the way I see it, it's the job of today's humans to get the place ready for them.

Sean Landis, born 2060.
Future mailperson to Mars.

Raheem Solanki, born 2032.
Future self-driving car mechanic

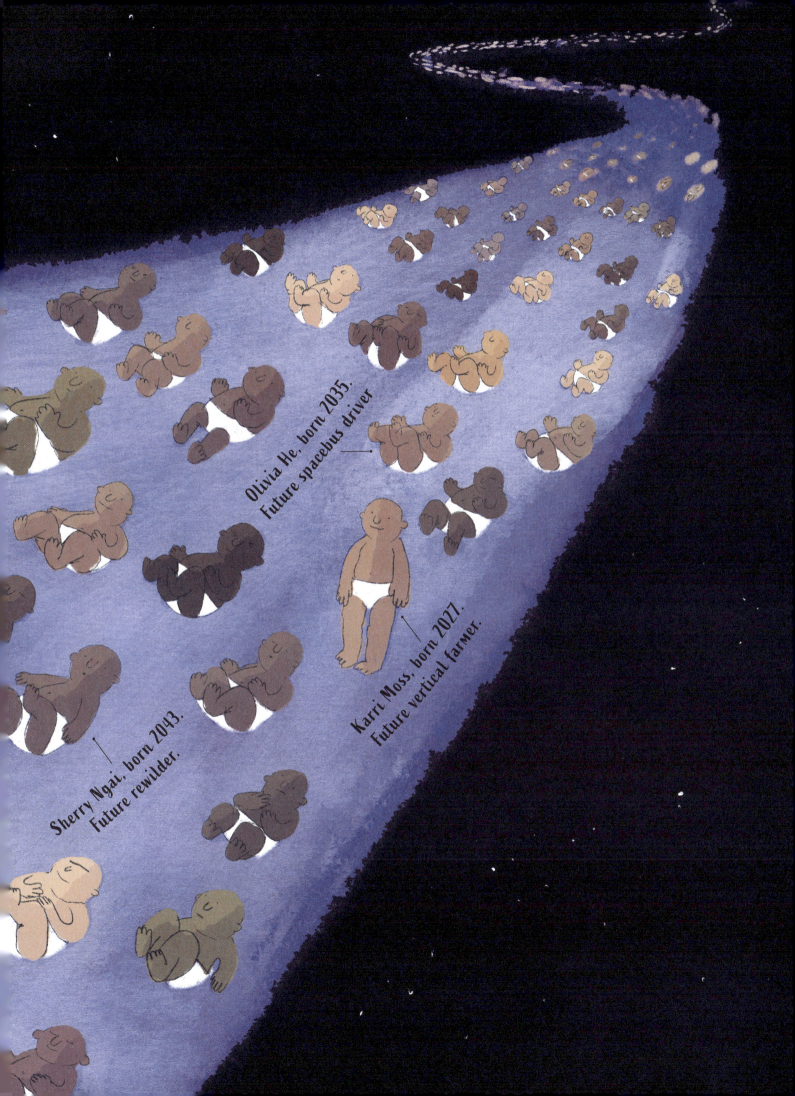

Olivia He, born 2035.
Future spacebus driver

Karri Moss, born 2027.
Future vertical farmer.

Sherry Ngai, born 2043.
Future rewilder.

Thinking long-term like a tree might not always come naturally. But I've known many humans who've done things for people they'd never live to meet . . .

like the stonemasons who began work on my church, which took over 100 years to finish,

1600

1820

the creators of the park and museum across the street (from what I hear, people are still enjoying them now),

1870

VOTES FOR WOMEN

VOTES FOR WOMEN

and these marchers, who began a campaign that ended up taking half a century. Many of them never got to vote, but their granddaughters did.

Today, there are people all over the world doing things
especially for the humans of the future.

Like the forest guardians who've spent
their whole lives planting trees
(and training others to do the same),

the indigenous people who think seven
generations ahead in their big decisions,

or the scientists keeping all kinds of seeds safe for a thousand years
in seed banks, so future humans can regrow rare plants.

When you think about it, there are all kinds of ways human beings can shape what's next.

It's as if you can travel through time and help out people who haven't even been born yet.

You could plant a seed that becomes a tree . . .

that a future human climbs someday.

You could pass down a story that others share . . .

that becomes a movie and spreads some more.

You could write a book that doesn't sell . . .

only for future readers to discover a classic.

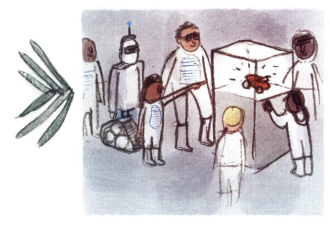

You could look after
a toy so well . . .

that one day, museumgoers
will line up for a look.

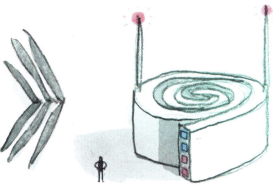

You could teach someone, who'll
grow up to teach someone else . . .

who'll invent . . . this thing.

You could help build a house . . .

that one family after another
will call their home.

Not many species can do that. Maybe it's your superpower.

If you could see time the way I do, you'd realize that you're all part of the same story, stretching backward and forward for thousands of years.

You're all connected by what you pass on.

You ought to be going.
I expect you've got human things to do.
And I've been rambling on.

But if you ever need to slow down and marvel at
the past, breathe in the present, or dream about
the future, find an old tree.

There's probably one nearer than you think.

Come and sit with us.

Tell us what's on your mind.

We're excellent listeners.

We're not in a hurry.

To our dad, who was never rushed.

LAURENCE KING
First published in the United States in 2025 by
Laurence King

HB ISBN: 978-1-510-23164-1
E-book ISBN: 978-1-510-23121-4

1 3 5 7 9 10 8 6 4 2

Printed in China

Laurence King
An imprint of
Hachette Children's Group
Part of Hodder and Stoughton
Carmelite House
50 Victoria Embankment
London EC4Y 0DZ

An Hachette UK Company
www.hachette.co.uk
www.hachettechildrens.co.uk
www.laurenceking.com